D0048589

THESE ARE

THE ANSWERS!

(The Questions are on the back cover...)

1. Nothing!

2. Drunk!

3. Between Joe and Sadie!

4. Joe and Sadie!

5. Open Manhole!

6. December 13, 1938

7. Not buying this thrilling book.

Don't *YOU* make the same mistake!

More **MAD** Humor from **SIGNET**

- [ ] **MAD'S DAVE BERG LOOKS AT PEOPLE**
  (#P3717—60¢)
- [ ] **MAD'S DAVE BERG LOOKS AT THINGS**
  (#P3718—60¢)
- [ ] **MAD'S DAVE BERG LOOKS AT THE U.S.A.**
  (#P3715—60¢)

**by Dick De Bartolo, Jack Davis and
Mort Drucker**

- [ ] **A MAD LOOK AT OLD MOVIES**   (#P3702—60¢)

by William M. Gaines

- [ ] **THE BEDSIDE MAD**   (#P3520—60¢)
- [ ] **BOILING MAD**   (#P3523—60¢)
- [ ] **BURNING MAD**   (#P3610—60¢)
- [ ] **FIGHTING MAD**   (#P3714—60¢)
- [ ] **GOOD 'N' MAD**   (#P3824—60¢)
- [ ] **GREASY MAD STUFF**   (#P3522—60¢)
- [ ] **HOWLING MAD**   (#P3613—60¢)
- [ ] **THE IDES OF MAD**   (#P3492—60¢)
- [ ] **INDIGESTIBLE MAD**   (#P3477—60¢)
- [ ] **IT'S A WORLD, WORLD, WORLD, WORLD MAD**
  (#P3720—60¢)
- [ ] **LIKE MAD**   (#P3491—60¢)
- [ ] **THE MAD FRONTIER**   (#P3727—60¢)
- [ ] **MAD IN ORBIT**   (#P3494—60¢)
- [ ] **THE MAD SAMPLER**   (#P3495—60¢)
- [ ] **MAD'S SNAPPY ANSWERS TO STUPID QUESTIONS**
  (#P3555—60¢)
- [ ] **MAD'S SPY VS. SPY**   (#P3480—60¢)
- [ ] **THE ORGANIZATION MAD**   (#P3728—60¢)
- [ ] **THE QUESTIONABLE MAD**   (#P3719—60¢)
- [ ] **RAVING MAD**   (#P3490—60¢)
- [ ] **THE SELF-MADE MAD**   (#P3716—60¢)
- [ ] **THE VOODOO MAD**   (#P3521—60¢)
- [ ] **VIVA MAD**   (#P3516—60¢)

**THE NEW AMERICAN LIBRARY, INC., P.O. Box 2310, Grand
Central Station, New York, New York 10017**

Please send me the SIGNET BOOKS I have checked above. I
am enclosing $_____(check or money order—no
currency or C.O.D.'s). Please include the list price plus 10¢ a
copy to cover mailing costs. (New York City residents add 6%
Sales Tax. Other New York State residents add 3% plus any
local sales or use taxes.)

Name_____

Address_____

City_____State_____Zip Code_____

Allow at least 3 weeks for delivery.

THE RETURN OF A  LOOK AT OLD MOVIES

Screenplay by **DICK DE BARTOLO**

Cinematography by **JACK DAVIS**

Directed by **NICK MEGLIN**

A SIGNET BOOK from

NEW AMERICAN LIBRARY

TIMES MIRROR

New York and Toronto
The New English Library Limited, London

For all those dinners that got cold while I worked
without complaint . . .
For all those wonderful suggestions humbly made . . .
For all those long hours of waiting without remorse . . .
This book is proudly dedicated . . .

TO WHOM IT MAY CONCERN!

Copyright © 1970 by Dick De Bartolo, Jack Davis,
and E. C. Publications

All rights reserved

SIGNET TRADEMARK REG. U.S. PAT. OFF. AND FOREIGN COUNTRIES
REGISTERED TRADEMARK—MARCA REGISTRADA
HECHO EN CHICAGO, U.S.A.

SIGNET BOOKS are published *in the United States* by
The New American Library, Inc.,
1301 Avenue of the Americas, New York, New York 10019,
in Canada by The New American Library of Canada Limited
295 King Street East, Toronto 2, Ontario,
in the United Kingdom by The New English Library Limited,
Barnard's Inn, Holborn, London, E.C. 1, England

FIRST PRINTING, MARCH, 1970

PRINTED IN THE UNITED STATES OF AMERICA

Contents

"THE BIGGEST TOP ON EARTH"   9

An electrifying plot ends up in a short *circus*!

"LIFE DINGHY"   35

This movie is rated *sea*!

"THE CASE OF THE MAN WHO DIED A LOT"   53

Another *stiff*!

"PERISCOPES OUT OF THE BLUE"   85

Another sub-standard standard *sub* movie!

"THE INVENTING FOOL"   109

You can't con *Edison*!

"FLIGHT 1313"   129

A *plane* old Hollywood story!

"BLAZING BLADES"   151

A *sworded* affair!

"CAMPUS CAPERS"   179

Rah rah! Sis boom *blah*!

FOREWORD

There is always great interest in book authors, and it's both an honor and a privilege to be selected by this author to write a short biography about him for this book. To be chosen for this, in view of my humble background, just goes to show that where else but in a country like ours can an orphan like myself, wretched and poor, pick himself up by his bootstraps and rise above his environment to the point where he can be even *considered* to write a foreword about a man like the author of this book. It wasn't easy, I'll clue you. I mean, how would *you* like to be the only kid out of an orphanage class of 45 that wasn't chosen by foster parents? No, I'm sure you wouldn't like it either. "Too sensitive," I would hear them whisper as they took their Johnnies and Jimmies back to their warm homes and chocolate cake. "Too shy," they would say as that fink Harvey Stonebreaker climbed on a new Schwinn bike his new foster parents bought him. Well, I don't need *anyone* to buy me a bike, Harvey Stonebreaker, wherever you are! I hope you're reading this so you'll know that I made it! I can buy all the bikes I want! With money I earned writing, Harvey! Writing things like forewords for important people like the author of this book, Harvey. People who wouldn't have *anything* to do with the likes of *you!*

But I've gotten off the subject a bit, haven't I? I guess you want to know what happened to me *after* I left the orphanage. Well, I was 18, and I got this job writing scenarios for a stag film producer. My award winning film, "The Plumber's Apprentice," caught the attention of the publisher of Mad Magazine, and, well, here I am

I've certainly enjoyed this opportunity to write about the author of this book, a real great guy.

nick meglin

Associate Editor
Mad Magazine

THE BIGGEST TOP ON EARTH

Laydees and gennelmunn . . . in the center ringgg on the high weyer . . . the gareatest trapeez act in the universe . . . The Balancing Bumblers from Babylon . . . working tonight **without a safety net yet . . .**
Who gave them permission to work without a **net?** You know what happened to the **last act** that tried that!

Yeah, it was the **"Dozen Daredevils"** one night and **"Three On A Bike"** the next. But boy did they have **guts!**

I know. It took **hours** to clean the place up!

There isn't a sound under the big top as this marvelous troupe starts to build toward their death-defying finale . . . even the **slightest sound** could disturb the deep concentration necessary for successful wire maneuverability . . .

Oh, I don't know. I just like wearing it, I guess. Ever since I was a boy of 15 I've been wearing make-up. You know how it is . . .

I know how it is if you're a **girl** of 15, but a boy, I'm afraid, has some problems. It isn't that you're trying to **hide** from someone, is it Rolley?

Hide from someone? What kind of crack is **that!** You certainly know how to hurt a clown!

I'm sorry, Rolley. I've been in too many circus movies where the clown wears make-up to hide from the law and I just figured this was **another** one. How could I have been so wrong? You've got such an **honest face** . . .

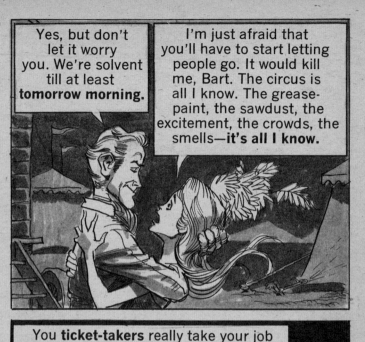

Yes, but don't let it worry you. We're solvent till at least **tomorrow morning.**

I'm just afraid that you'll have to start letting people go. It would kill me, Bart. The circus is all I know. The grease-paint, the sawdust, the excitement, the crowds, the smells—**it's all I know.**

You **ticket-takers** really take your job **seriously,** don't you? Well, don't worry, Margo. Your job is secure. Till **morning,** anyway . . . HEY! Do you smell smoke?

Why, yes . . .

Well, this is still not the end! As long as there's **one costume** left . . . as long as there's **one pole** to hold up a piece of canvas . . . as long as there's **one ticket** to sell . . . we're going to have a **show**!

Here's, the report on the damage Bart. There's **not one costume** left, **not one pole** to hold up a piece of canvas, and **all the tickets** have been burned to a crisp.

Bart, the gang is proud of you. A little while ago we were discussing your problems and we said to ourselves "Wouldn't it be a nice gesture to pool all our cash and sell what little we had and turn the money over to you" . . .

Please, Jingo, I'm deeply moved, but that would be **too much.** However . . .

That's what we thought too, so we **didn't do it!**

Thanks **loads!** But what I said still goes— we're going to all pitch in and see this thing through. We're going to have a show **tonight!**

Laydees and gennelmunn . . . welcome to the Ring-a-ding Bros. Circus. Even though we are missing a costume or two, we hope you will enjoy tonight's performances.

To start us off tonight in a dazzling display of horsemanship and marksmanship is our manager, Bart Baker himself! Bart will ride a fast galloping horse around the ring while **shooting light bulbs** out of the mouths of our clown troupe . . .

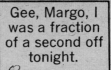

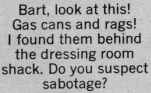

LIFE·DINGHY

Now, attention passengers. You all realize that our ship has sunk and that there are nine of us in this lifeboat which has a capacity for four. Needless to say, things will not be as pleasant as they were when we were back on the ship. First of all, there'll be Bingo only twice a week . . .

Boo . . . Boo . . .

There will be only one sitting for dinner!

You mean to say the first class passengers will have to eat with the tourist class passengers?

Madam, the first class passengers may have to eat the tourist class passengers!

45

You just want to hear more prayers . . . Well it won't work, Jonas.

Tell me, Mrs. Lilac, why did you decide to take this ill-fated cruise.

It was my children's idea. I'm getting on in years . . . and well, I was getting in the way . . . You know how old folks suddenly seem to be in the way with the younger ones. So they sent me away.

How mean of them! Now, Mrs. Lilac, would you please be a good little old lady, and jump over the side. I'm afraid you're in the way . . .

48

The Case Of
THE MAN
WHO
DIED A LOT

54

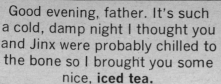

57

Thank you, Jinx. You know, it's funny that modern science had not thought of rebuilding the human body a long time ago. After all, the heart is only a pump, the arteries are just tubes, the brain merely a storage cell . . .

What are you going to use to replace the **liver?**

So far I've been using a bag of **marshmallows.** It doesn't quite work like a liver, but it certainly **feels** the same . . .

All right, in there. Open up. This is the **police!**

Egads! The police! My daughter really reported me! They'll give me the **gas chamber** . . . or maybe **worse** — take away my **driver's license!**

Open up or we'll blow the house down!

Not by the hair on my chinny-chin-chin!

Jinx, quickly. Go out through the **secret panel.** If they execute me, claim my body and bring me **back to life.** Take these books—they have all my notes. The last one is the most important . . . the one to the milkman telling him to **stop delivery!**

61

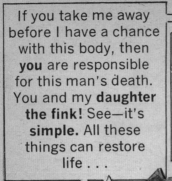

If you take me away before I have a chance with this body, then **you** are responsible for this man's death. You and my **daughter the fink!** See—it's **simple.** All these things can restore life . . .

That's insanity! A pump, some chemicals, tubes . . . and what's this bag of **gum drops** for?

Put that **pancreas** down!

You'd better come along quietly, doctor . . .

MAD SCIENTIST ARRESTED
Doctor Fear Found In Laboratory With Body. Fink Daughter Leads Police to Scene

MAD SCIENTIST GOES TO TRIAL
Daughter Will Act As Witness For D.A. Green Hornet Still at Large

50¢ THE DAILY P

MAD SCIENTIST DIES TONIGHT IN GAS CHAMBER
Fear Has No Fear. Says "I've had gas pains before!"

THE MORNIN

FRIDAY 13, 1969

I CAUGHT

65

Doctor Fear was my closest fiend, er, **friend.** He would have wanted me to have something to **remember him by,** like his body.

My good man, do you think you can just march in off the street and claim a body **just like that?** Though it is extinguished, it is not something one gives away. It is still a wonderful mechanism . . .

Here's five dollars . . .

Take **all you want!**

Now you can prove to the world that you were not insane; that you can bring back the dead!

No!!! I want no one to know of this. Society had damned me to death, and now I am **legally dead.** I cannot be held responsible for anything I do. I can rob, torture, kill, and not even return library books—and no one can touch me!

Doctor, you are talking like a **mad-man.** You've made a brilliant discovery. You must share it with the world.   If **you** don't tell them about it, **I will!**

Hey, world! Listen to me for a minute!

75

Well, there's something mighty strange going on. **All** the 40 people killed in this insane murder spree played some part in the execution of your father. I think it's part of some fiendish plot. I think your father's experiments in bringing back life might have **succeeded.** I think your father is **still alive** and is responsible for those murders.

Quit beating around the bush and tell me what you **think!**

I think we should go back to the laboratory and search for a **secret room** your father may be hiding in.

And if he's not there we can always **neck . . .**

79

Sure, but why bother to **raise** a few kids? We can **make** them! After all, the heart is only a **pump,** the arteries are just **tubes...**

Periscopes
Out of the
Blue

Why don't you stop **copying** me and think of your **own** clever things to say, Lieutenant? Tomorrow I'm going to let **you** talk first and **I'll** copy you! **Then** you'll see how hard it is being a Captain!

Yes, yes, what's all the fuss and bother about?

It's Fishman, Captain. He has **acute appendicitis**...

I don't care if he has a cute appendicitis or **adorable adenoids,** I need him at his station. Every man has a job on this ship and no one can be **replaced, least of all** Fishman! He's the only **laundry room man** in the Navy who knows how to keep **shorty pajamas** soft and comfy!

But Captain, unless his appendix is removed immediately, Fishman will **die.** And we don't have a **doctor** on board.

If he dies, you don't **need** a doctor, silly! And as Pharmacist's Mate, **you** must know what to do . . .

I don't have the **instruments,** the **operating table,** the **sterilization equipment,** and with Fishman not at his job, I don't even have **clean sheets!**

We'll leave the choice to **him . . .**

Listen, Hank, I know you're in pain, but you **gotta** hear me. It's **your** choice to make! Either Gordon here **operates,** or we put you in a torpedo tube and **shoot you over** to a ship with a doctor. What'll it be, boy?

I'll take my chances with **Gordon,** Sir. I've **heard** about your aim with the torpedoes!

THE INVENTING FOOL

110

111

112

I knew the day would someday come when my little boy would become a man and fly the coop. But I won't be sad. Time will mend a mother's broken heart, and before long I'll soon forget all about . . . . er, **what's** his name . . . .

ROOM FOR RENT

Hey, what's this stuff? It looks like potassium nitrate, acetic acid, common mold . . . . you're not allowed to **experiment** on a train!

Who's experimenting? This is **apple pie!** You know how lousy food is on a train!

And so, Tom Edison began his work. But this time as a man, and not as a boy. And his mother encouraged him as a man, and not as a boy, which didn't help his Oedipus complex too much! She rented him back his room where he worked 24 hours a day, sometimes even longer . . .

Tom, this is ridiculous. You've been working too long, too hard. You don't even stop to **eat.** Let me **sell** you a bowl of soup . . .

I can't stop now. I have to **perfect** this latest experiment!

What's to **perfect?** That thing has been burning brightly for days now. It's a perfect **electric light bulb!**

It's supposed to be a **telephone!**

Then like so . . . .

And like so again! Why let them pay once for this when you can make them pay for **each of these** along the way! That, Mother, is science! The science of **making a bundle!**

118

Unwilling to bend with progress and reluctant to accept new-fangled gadgets, the townspeople tormented poor Tom . . .

Look at them out there. Fools! If they would only listen to me they wouldn't be out there with torches and rocks — they'd be out there with **electric lights and rocks!**

He's a witch! Burn him!

He's a maniac! Jail him!

He's uncouth! Couth him!

But Tom continued his work and soon began to amaze his associates with one invention after another . . .

121

122

Tom began lecturing on his theory of generating electricity . . .

Gentlemen, strange as it sounds, I actually **generate electricity** when I pet this cat!

Mr. Edison, will the electricity generated be powerful enough to do anything?

No. And this is where all of you can help me. We need a greater source of power to produce enough electrical force to harness and utilize. Do any of you know where I can get a **15 foot pussy cat?**

Preposterous!

Tom, more determined than ever, began his endless work once again . . .

FLIGHT 1313

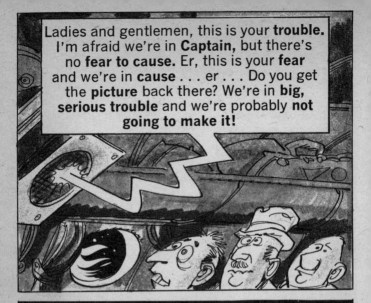

You did that before we **left the ground,** remember? You pulled the extinguisher knob thinking it was the **windshield wipers . . .**

It's **your** fault, McGee! There are 200 damn switches in this cockpit. I know about **half** of them. If **you** were any kind of a co-pilot you'd learn the **rest of them** and we would be a real **team!**

Suppose we **cut the fuel** going to engines #3 and 4?

If you do that, they won't run. Bet you thought you'd **catch me** on that trick question!

You co-pilots are **power hungry,** do you know that, McGee? It's time to sit and wait and hope and think back about the events that brought us to this crucial, suspenseful moment! Can't you see the FLASHBACK indicator lighting up? **Every** Hollywood-built plane has one!

Oh, I see. My thoughts are drifting back . . . back to Dorothy. Before we took off I was thinking of walking out on her and the 10 kids. But if we make it out of this alive, I'm going back to her. I might even **marry** her. Bachelor life has been no fun with 10 kids. . . .

137

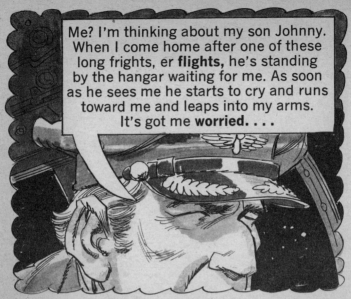

Me? I'm thinking about my son Johnny. When I come home after one of these long frights, er **flights,** he's standing by the hangar waiting for me. As soon as he sees me he starts to cry and runs toward me and leaps into my arms. It's got me **worried. . . .**

Worried? What on earth for? That sounds **wonderful!**

Johnny's **27 years old!**

I see what you mean. But I think we've spent **enough time** on our own flashbacks, Captain. Shouldn't we go back to the cabin and pick up the thoughts of some of the **passengers?**

By God, McGee, you're catching on **fast!** We'll make a Hollywood pilot out of you yet!

138

Boy, is this ironic . . . I embezzle a half million dollars and then take a plane heading for disaster. A half million dollars! What can it buy up here? Can it buy me a **safe landing?** Hah! It's now in HIS hands. Only HE can decide if I'll live or die. Only HE can make the difference, but you can't buy HIM with money. Not a lousy **half million,** anyway . . .
WALL STREET JOURNAL

I was going to **divorce** Harry. I didn't want to be **tied down** anymore. That's a laugh! Here I am, Audrey Tawdry on a flight to freedom, and the person I miss **most** is Harry. If I get out of this alive, I'm **going back** to Harry. And I'm never going to mention freedom to him again! I'll just **sneak out** nights without his knowing it. . . .

What a joke! I desert from the Army because I'm a **coward.** I'm afraid to face the possibility of dying. So what do I do? I get on a plane facing death! If I get out of this alive I'm **going back** to my Company and sign up for a **dangerous mission**—like Recruiting at the Berkeley campus . . .

I planned the **perfect crime** and got away with it. I murdered my **nagging wife** and made it look like **her mother** did it! If **that** isn't the perfect crime, what is? But now that I face death, I realize how **selfish** I've been. I only thought of **me.** If I survive this, I'm going to **make it up** to them. I'll send flowers to the **grave** and cookies to the **penitentiary . . .**

I haven't done my **job.** I haven't done all I could have. And now that I face impending doom, I realize I have not set an example to those around me. If we land safely, I'm starting off on a **clean slate.** I'm going to go to church next Sunday. And **every** Sunday from then on. After all, I am a **minister. . . .**

Attention, ladies and gentlemen. This is the Captain. While you were all having your **revealing thoughts,** the two fires went out and we were able to locate a small airfield in the area. The landing is going to be **rough** and **dangerous.** When the plane is in **perfect condition** my landings are rough and dangerous, so you can imagine what **this** one's going to be like! Hang on, cause **here we go. . . .**

145

148

BLAZING
BLADES

153

Well, Captain Blood . . . **soaking wet** again! Lose **another** ship?
No, I hid it at the bottom of the ocean where no one can find it. Now be quiet, you **wrench!**
That's **wench!** There's someone waiting to see you in the **north booth . . .**
YE END

That's **swashbuckler.** I'll get right to the point. If you'll do a little job for me, I'll provide you with another ship. The daughter of the Duke of Fricasse, Lady Lasagna, is leaving the Chateau Croissant for Turkey aboard the Golden Goose . . .

Do you mind if I **order some food?** I'm suddenly very **hungry . . .**

Lady Lasagna is wearing a certain **gold locket** that I want. This is an **exact replica** of it. You are to intercept her ship and switch lockets without her knowing. When you return with it, I will hand you the ownership papers of the ship you will be sailing.

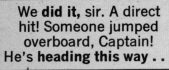

160

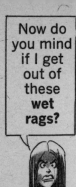

Now do you mind if I get out of these **wet rags**?

You can change into these **dry rags** if you'd like. They belong to the first mate, but it's **all we have!**

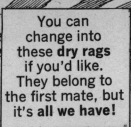

Do you mind **closing your eyes** while I slip into them, please?

Why don't you **close yours!** Thay way you won't see us watching and we'll **all** be happy! . . .

Captain! You're **insubordinate!**

Since you pay me a **compliment**, my lady, I will turn around . . .

163

167

171

173

Well, this is where I live! **Duel me out . . .**

WELCOME TO TWITTERMOUNT

And where does the **locket** fit into all of this?

The locket did **not** come from the mail-order house as legend has it. It was mine, given to me **at birth.** My twin brother also had one, but he was kidnapped by a wandering gypsy group who adopted him by inflicting the "Mark of Gnocchi," a scar that goes across the back, up, over the shoulder, around the neck and down again under the arm . . .

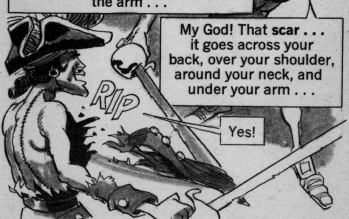

RIP

My God! That **scar** . . . it goes across your back, over your shoulder, around your neck, and under your arm . . .

Yes!

175

CAMPUS CAPERS

183

Frank and Barbara, get ready for your **locomotive** number. Dave, you got the **cattle** ready for the "Rodeo Stampede" sketch? Joan, when you do the dream sequence in the "Fly To Love" number with Stan, don't stand too close to the **propeller** We've already lost Jonas! Bill, you blowing up the **zeppelin?** Good! Arnie, check out the **harem girls** for the "Ali Baba" number!